READING MY ARSE!

Hot on the heels of the hugely popular books Football My Arse! and Celebrities My Arse! comes an exciting, off-beat novel by Ricky Tomlinson, the much-loved comedy actor who doubles as a bestselling author.

Inspired by Ricky's love of reading, this is the thrilling story of one young man's quest to cross the Atlantic from Liverpool in search of the Rock Island Line, the legendary American railway line, and follows the adventures that change his life for ever.

READING MY ARSE!

Searching for the Rock Island Line

A Novel

Ricky Tomlinson

with Norman Giller

SHORTLIST

First published in 2007
by Sphere
This Large Print edition published
2007 by BBC Audiobooks by
arrangement with
Little Brown Book Group

ISBN 978 1 405 62215 8

Printed and bound in Great Britain by
Antony Rowe Ltd., Chippenham, Wiltshire

Remembering Eileen and Clifton
with a smile

PREFACE

I owe so much to reading. In fact, I can say that reading changed me for the better and gave me the confidence to improve myself at what was a time of crisis in my life.

It's no secret that I lost a couple of years of my life to a prison sentence that, I swear, was a miscarriage of justice. [Ricky Tomlinson was sentenced to two years' imprisonment in 1973 for allegedly conspiring to cause an affray while organising union pickets on the building site where he worked as a plasterer. Ricky, now established as a best-selling author and one of our best-loved comedy actors, has always fiercely maintained his innocence.] It was the biggest stitch-up since the Bayeux Tapestry.

While banged up, I found the best way to make time pass was to lose myself in my imagination. I fantasised about what I would do when I got my freedom back.

One idea that kept floating round in my head was to write a story about a young man from Liverpool who becomes obsessed by the lyrics of a song and gets led on an adventure by them. Little did I think I had the slightest chance of getting the story published. But now, thanks to Quick Reads, I can share it with you, and if you enjoy it and it gives you the hunger to read another book, I will be dead chuffed.

Reading is a free gift for everybody. It broadens the mind even more than travel, and it can set you off on a never-ending journey of discovery. Please, please, keep reading, and I promise it will make you a more complete, more confident, more satisfied and better-informed person.

Don't let so-called pals sneer at you for picking up books and reading them from cover to cover. You will find the books become your best friends, and give you a whole new outlook on the world. Books kept me sane in prison. I was able to escape— not literally, of course—to places far beyond the four walls of my cell.

There is a lot of me in the hero of this book, and I hope the story captures what it was like to be part of the music revolution that swept through Liverpool in the late 1950s and into the 1960s with the arrival of the Beatles. If I'd had my way, I'd have jumped on the Beatles' bandwagon and followed them to Hamburg to help spread the Mersey Sound.

Hope you won't think I'm blowing my own trumpet (and I'm not referring to my big conk), but I have always been a storyteller. Even as a kid at school I could make an essay come alive with my imagination, which used to run riot. The actor in me was also let loose. I could hold my classmates spellbound with tales that came off the top of my head. And it was all inspired by the written word.

Yes, Reading My Arse!

It's not only books you should read. I used to devour the *Liverpool Echo* when I was a kid, starting at the back with all the football news about my heroes at Anfield (and I spared a glance for the Everton news, too!).

I was also heavily into reading comics. In those days there was a huge choice, ranging from *Topper*, *Film Fun* and, of course, the *Beano* and *Dandy*, to comics aimed at older kids like the *Hotspur*, the *Eagle* and the *Wizard*. But my personal favourite was the *Champion*, which didn't sell as much as the rest, and it concentrated more on the written word than illustrated stories. It was packed with adventure yarns, and the one I looked forward to reading each week featured a boxer called Rockfist Rogan. It started a life-long love affair for me with the fight game.

That was the result of reading about the sport.

And it was reading that made me want to be a writer. I used to read books like *Black Beauty* and *Treasure Island*, and almost ached to be able to write those sorts of adventure tales.

But at that time, where I came from, if I had let on that I wanted to be something as 'arty farty' as a writer, they would have ridiculed me. The phrase used in those days was 'getting an idea above your station'. So I stupidly kept my mouth shut, and failed to ask the teachers to help me realise my ambition.

You don't have to be rich to become a regular reader, but you will be richer for the experience. All you have to do is join your local library, and there will be shelves upon shelves of books just waiting for you. Yes, a feast awaits you once you decide that reading can be not only informative but also fun. And it will cost you nothing.

I picked up reading again when I was sent to prison, the worst time of my life yet strangely the one in which I grabbed the opportunity to better myself.

I read anything and everything while I was banged up. The book that made the greatest impression on me was *The Ragged Trousered Philanthropists* by Robert Tressell. If you get half a chance to read it, I beg you to take it. It tells the story of a group of builders and tradesmen in the fictional English town of Mugsborough in the early 1900s, and captures the class struggle of that period in a way that will hold you magnetised to the page.

That was my peak reading experience. Once again my desire to write was ignited by reading, and out of it has come the story you are now holding in your hands and, I hope, are about to enjoy.

So please come with me back to a past that remains rich in my memory. The time: the late 1950s. The place: Liverpool. This was when the Beatles were just about to strum their first chords, when rock 'n' roll was in its infancy and competing for popularity with a raw music called skiffle.

The cell door bangs closed, and I am alone with my imagination.

Ricky Tomlinson

CHAPTER ONE

Eric's winkle-pickers were a size too small and pinched his toes as he walked along Scotland Road, his hands deep in his pockets, deep in debt, deep in thought and with a deep depression fogging his brain like a Mersey mist.

He was on a losing streak. Carole, his latest girlfriend, had chucked him. He had just got the chop from his trainee sales manager's job, and—worst of all—the Reds had just been beaten by Everton. True, it was only a reserves match. But any defeat of Liverpool by their detested neighbours was like a slash on the wrist.

The only way things could get worse was if somebody stole his pride and joy, a 125cc Vespa scooter that he had bought second-hand from Carole's brother for fifty quid.

That was five weeks' wages, borrowed in advance, but it was worth every penny to know the freedom of the road. He had chained the scooter to the Stanley Park railings while he went to the footie match.

The Vespa was still there. It was only when he leaned over to unchain it that he realised somebody had stolen the front wheel. Eric was now in deep despair.

As he started to push the one-wheeled scooter home, little did he know that this was going to be the day that changed his life.

A ragged-arsed kid laughed as he watched Eric pushing the scooter along the pavement. 'Hey, mister,' he shouted in thick Scouse, 'you're supposed to ride dem tings. It's not a pram, y'know.'

'Sod off, you little scally,' Eric spat back, 'or you'll go home wearing your testicles as a bow tie.' Only he didn't say testicles.

As the scallywag scurried off laughing, Eric pushed the scooter past a second-hand and part-exchange shop, where the shopkeeper was preparing to put up the shutters.

Eric did a double-take as he looked in the window. Hanging from a hook was a highly polished, six-stringed Spanish guitar. It had a sheet of paper stuck to it, on which was written: 'Identical to the guitar played by Lonnie Donegan. Yours for £15.'

Lonnie Donegan, the King of Skiffle, was Eric's current idol.

Purely on impulse, Eric said to the shopkeeper: 'What would you give me for this scooter?'

The shopkeeper, who had a heavily lined, saggy bag-of-spanners face, puffed out his cheeks, then sucked on his teeth as he studied the wounded scooter like a judge at a dog show.

'You're asking me to quote you a

price for a one-legged chicken,' he said. 'I'd want you to pay me to get rid of it.'

'Be fair, pal,' Eric said, setting himself up for a little bargaining. 'I paid seventy-five quid for this just four months ago.'

'Seventy-five quid!' the shop-keeper exclaimed. 'Who sold it to you? Dick Turpin? You know *vespa* is Italian for "wasp" . . . well, you were stung.'

'It had two wheels until today,' Eric said, defensively. 'Some toerag stole the front wheel while I was at Goodison watching the match.'

'You Blue or Red?' the shopkeeper asked, suddenly eyeing Eric with suspicion.

'Red through and through,' said Eric.

The shopkeeper warmed a little. 'Just as well,' he said. 'If you'd been a Blue, I'd have told you to bugger off.'

He made a closer study of the scooter. 'Tell you what I'll do,' he said, 'I'll give you a tenner to take it off your hands.'

Eric looked again at the guitar, his eyes drawn to it. The instrument seemed almost to be calling to him.

'How about,' he said, 'doing a swap—that guitar for this scooter.'

'D'you play?' asked the shopkeeper.

'Not yet,' said Eric, 'but my granddad's a magician on a banjo. He'll show me how.'

The shopkeeper one-wheeled the Vespa into a storeroom and returned with a black guitar case. 'This case is worth as much as that bloody scooter,' he said, as he took the guitar out of the window and placed it inside.

As Eric took the case he felt as made up as if he was being given the crown jewels.

'Oh yes,' said the shopkeeper, 'one more thing. The fella I bought the guitar off left this in the case. You might as well have it.'

He handed Eric the sheet music for Lonnie Donegan's hit skiffle song, 'Rock Island Line'.

As he walked out of the shop, the elated Eric had the strange feeling he was somehow holding his destiny in his hands.

CHAPTER TWO

Over the next year Eric and his guitar were inseparable. He called it Bessie, after Liverpool's legendary MP Bessie Braddock, and wherever Eric went, Bessie was sure to go.

The fingertips on his left hand were red sore from finding all the different chords on the neck of the guitar as he practised night and day. His granddad George was a self-taught banjoist, who had learned to play while sailing the seven seas. He was a born comedian, and his Mersey wit lit up many a pub drinking session. 'The secret of getting a girl in every port,' he used to say, 'is to get a port into every girl.' He was known as 'Signpost' because his arms and much of his body were covered in tattoos featuring the names of all the countries he had visited as a merchant seaman.

'Australia' was just above his arse—Down Under, he called it—and 'Liverpool' ran in a circle round his heart. He kidded people that he had 'India' tattooed on his penis, and that in moments of great excitement it read 'Indianapolis'.

Granddad George was Eric's mentor, the wisest man he knew. He lived next door in a two-up two-down and you could hardly move in there for books. The walls were lined with bookcases he had made, and books spilled out of almost every drawer and cupboard. He refused to let go of any book he had read. 'It would be like letting go of a good friend,' he said.

There were books on every subject you could think of, and many of them were brought home from his many voyages during fifty years as a seaman.

For a man who had left school at fourteen barely able to read, the range of his knowledge was amazing. He did his best to pass on as much of it as possible to his only grandson. 'Knowledge gleaned from books is like a relay baton,' he used to say, 'and it's your duty to pass it on. Just remember this, Eric lad: if you learn the meaning of just one new word every day, by the end of the year you will have increased your vocabulary by three hundred and sixty-five words, and in ten years time you will be a walking, talking dictionary.'

Granddad George willingly gave Eric lessons to help him find basic chords, and with the further support of guitar guru Bert Weedon's *Play In A Day* tuition book, he quickly began to strum to a reasonably good standard.

Eric was pleasantly surprised to find that his once lead-choirboy-soprano voice had come down the scale to a fairly gruff baritone, which ideally suited the skiffle songs he copied note for note from his collection of 45rpm records featuring Lonnie Donegan.

It was an amazing time to be a young musician in Liverpool. In virtually every Merseyside street there were kids getting together to make music. A lot of it was borrowed from the United States, from where the first pounding beat of rock 'n' roll was crossing the Atlantic on records made by the likes of Bill Haley and his Comets, Little Richard and a young hip-swivelling singer called Elvis Presley.

All over Liverpool groups were being formed, like Rory Storm and the Hurricanes, who featured Ringo Starr on the drums. They were rock 'n' rollers to their boots, while a rival band called The Quarrymen had more of a skiffle influence. They had joint lead singers called John Lennon and Paul McCartney. The Beatles had yet to be born.

Lonnie Donegan, along with Wally Whyton and the Vipers, was leading the skiffle movement, which had its roots in jazz and blues and folk music rather than rock 'n' roll. Chas McDevitt and Nancy Whiskey were also pushing the skiffle rhythms on a popular BBC television programme called *Six-Five Special*, with a young Cliff Richard and Liverpool idol Billy Fury spreading the rival Elvis-style sounds. It was rock versus skiffle. Eric had no doubt that skiffle was the road to travel.

Eric got together with two old school pals to form the Rock Island Skifflers. He was lead singer and guitarist, Alan 'Sherlock' Holmes was on tea-chest bass and Terry 'The Terror' Thompson was on washboard. They had all been born in 1940, so were the first of their generation to miss National Service because the cut-off birth date for call-up was 31 December 1939. The two years they would have spent in the army were instead focused on being part of the Mersey Beat explosion. Eric knew that if there had still been National Service, the many groups getting together across the United Kingdom—and in particular in Liverpool—would probably never have been formed. He much preferred the prospect of finding chords to firing bullets.

The Rock Island Skifflers were rehearsing in a room above the Grafton, a ballroom that attracted Saturday-night dancers, when they got their first break. The Grafton manager invited them to play 'live' in the dancehall, and they went down a storm. They then got a regular booking, which pulled the jivers in. Their fifteen-pound fee was split three ways, a fiver each. They felt like real pros.

They started to earn a bit extra by supporting bands at places like the one-time jazz club cellar called the Cavern in Mathew Street and the Halfway House pub in Scotland Road. Alan Holmes and Terry Thompson soon graduated to playing a proper bass and drums. Eric fought against this because he was a skiffle purist at heart, and he felt that the tea-chest bass and washboard gave them an authentic look and sound.

It was with good reason that Terry Thompson was nicknamed 'The Terror'. He had a temper on him that could turn him from a likeable wise-cracker into a raving psychopath in the blink of an eye. He threatened to use his washboard to give Eric an extra parting in his Brylcreemed hair if he would not agree to him playing proper drums. Eric had to agree.

They always opened and closed

their set with the first song Eric had learned, 'Rock Island Line'. It was hardly challenging to him as a guitarist because there were just three chords—D-A-G. But because it had the rhythmic beat of a railway engine picking up speed, it always appealed to the jivers, who would go into dazzling spins as they got caught up in the increasing excitement and drive of the song. Eric had the words written on a huge card stuck on his bedroom wall. He could have sung and spoken them in his sleep, impersonating a 'Deep South' American accent in the same way as Lonnie Donegan . . .

SPOKEN, *with a steady beat*:
Now this here's the story about the
    Rock Island Line
Now, the Rock Island Line she
    runs down into New Orleans
And just outside of New Orleans
    there's a big toll-gate
And all the trains that go through

the toll-gate
Why, they gotta pay the man some
money
But, of course, if you've got certain
things on board
You're OK, you don't have to pay
the man nothin'
And just now we see a train, she
comin' down the line
When she come up near the toll-
gate
The driver, he shout down to the
man, and he say:

CHANT:
I got pigs, I got horses, I got cows
I got sheep, I got all livestock, I got
all livestock
I got all livestock

SPOKEN:
Hear man say, 'Well, you're all
right, boy,
Just get on through, you don't
have to pay me nothin''
And then the train go through

And when he go through the toll-
gate
The train got up a little bit of
steam
And a little bit of speed
And when the driver think he
safely on the other side
He shout back down the line to the
man, he said:

CHANT:
I fooled you, I fooled you
I got pig iron, I got pig iron
I got all pig iron

SPOKEN
'Now I tell you where I'm goin',
boy.'

CHORUS, *sung with a gradually
accelerating rhythm*:

Down the Rock Island Line, it is a
mighty good road
Oh, the Rock Island Line, it is the
road to ride

Oh, the Rock Island Line, it is a mighty good road
Well, if you want to ride you got to ride it like you find it
Get your ticket at the station for the Rock Island Line
I may be right, I may be wrong
You know you're gonna miss me when I'm gone
On the Rock Island Line
Hey you are safe within
The good Lord's a-comin' to see me again
A-B-C-W-X-Y-Zee
The cat's on the cover but he don't see me

REPEAT CHORUS, *gathering more pace*:

Now the Rock Island Line is a mighty good road
Oh the Rock Island Line is the road to ride
The Rock Island Line is a mighty good road

Well if you want to ride you gotta
　　ride it like you find it
Get your ticket at the station of
　　the Rock Island Line

Hallelujah, I'm safe from sin
The good Lord's a-comin'
For to see me again
Down the Rock Island Line

KEEP REPEATING THE CHORUS

Eric's granddad listened to him practising 'Rock Island Line' at home alone one day and got out his banjo and accompanied him, adding singing harmonies on the chorus.

'You've picked that up quickly, Granddad,' Eric said afterwards.

'I was singing that before you were born,' Granddad George said.

Eric laughed. 'Come off it,' he said. 'Lonnie Donegan only recorded it a couple of years ago.'

'You don't think that's a Lonnie Donegan original, do you?' his granddad said.

'It said in the *Melody Weekly* that he wrote the song,' Eric replied.

'Gollocks,' said Granddad. 'Wait here a minute.'

He went to his house next door and came back five minutes later with an old celluloid ten-inch 78rpm record clutched in his hand. Not surprising, Eric thought, that in America they called it a platter, and he wondered what music his granddad was about to play.

'Listen to this,' he said, placing the record on the old wind-up gramophone in Eric's bedroom with a clunk.

Eric was transfixed as he heard a crackling and obviously black man's voice coming from the gramophone, singing a slightly different but unmistakable version of 'Rock Island Line'. The song was much more bluesy than the Lonnie Donegan version, yet somehow more compelling and moving.

'Who's that singing, Granddad?' Eric asked after listening spellbound to the three-minute recording. 'It sounds as if it's been recorded in a lavvie.'

'That's the one and only Huddie Ledbetter,' said Granddad, proud to be able to show off his knowledge. 'He was nicknamed Lead Belly, and was the greatest guitar-playing blues singer that ever lived. Played a whopping great twelve-string guitar. That recording was made in prison in the 1930s when he was serving time.'

He produced an old, yellowing magazine cutting that had a picture of a wizened-looking Huddie Ledbetter strumming his twelve-string guitar, captioned: 'Leadbelly.' Granddad prodded it with a finger. 'That's the sort of sloppy journalism I can't stand,' he said. 'I know for sure Ledbetter was called Lead Belly—two words. I visited his grave in Louisiana on my last trip to the United States, and there it was as clear as anything, "Here lies Huddie 'Lead Belly' Ledbetter, a Louisiana Legend."'

'Where did you buy the record?' Eric asked, realising that it was a real collector's item.

'I bought it for two dollars in a record store in New York in 1947,' Granddad George explained. 'I've almost played it to death. That Lonnie Donegan version is just an imitation.'

'So the Rock Island Line really exists,' Eric said, making a statement rather than asking a question.

'Of course it does,' said Granddad. 'I've ridden it, and I suggest you should try to do the same thing.'

'How the heck do I manage that?' Eric asked.

He found himself both startled and excited by the reply. 'Do what I did, son,' said Granddad George. 'Join the Merchant Navy. Go and see the world.'

The advice was to change Eric's

life. Completely on impulse, he decided to take to the sea . . . at the start of a search for the Rock Island Line.

CHAPTER THREE

On 11 November 1960 Eric set sail for New York aboard the luxury liner *Britannic*. His granddad was a life member of the National Union of Seamen, and arranged that Eric could work as a kitchen hand while travelling on a United States visitor visa.

It was known as 'working your passage', and Eric found out just what real work was like after a year of unemployment on seven pounds a week dole money. The *Britannic* was heaving with fifteen hundred passengers on what was its final Liverpool-to-New York voyage after thirty years of transatlantic service, and on the six-day crossing Eric felt as if he was washing up for an army.

He rarely got a chance to see daylight away from the kitchen, and discovered just why it was known as the 'slave galley'. The chef allowed him one short break, when he managed to do a quick tour of the liner, looking in wonder at the worn, yet still striking, art deco fixtures and fittings that had given the ship its reputation for glamour and style.

The *Britannic* had been famously used as a troop ship during the Second World War, sailing nearly 400,000 miles and transporting more than 180,000 soldiers. She came home to Liverpool in 1947 and was converted back into a luxury passenger liner with a distinctive glassed-in promenade deck.

Even a month away from the breakers' yard, the *Britannic* was still a majestic sight. In the engine room the chief engineer proudly showed Eric what had been revolutionary machinery, the first diesel engines fitted on a major British ship.

Now the *Britannic* was heading for New York in what were historic days for the United States, which three days earlier had elected a new president in John F. Kennedy. There was a special president's ball on the third day of the crossing, and Eric sneaked away from the kitchen to stand backstage and watch the eight-piece band helping the passengers dance the night away. It made his fingers itch for Bessie, who was tucked away in her case in his tiny cabin.

He had managed to save one hundred pounds from the cash received for his gigs with the Rock Island Skifflers, which at the 1960 rate of exchange bought him 280 US dollars. Alan Holmes and Terry Thompson turned green with envy when he told them his plans to go to America to find the Rock Island Line. Both had wanted to join him, but were on the treadmill of mundane nine-to-five jobs. 'The working class,' Eric had joked, 'can kiss my arse. But don't worry, lads, when I get back from the States we'll make a fortune as full-time skifflers. It's the biggest craze since the hula hoop.'

'Yeah,' said the cynical Thompson, 'and that lasted all of five minutes.'

Eric spent what little spare time he got on the *Britannic* reading a series of articles his granddad had collected from *Jazz Monthly* and *Down Beat* on Huddie 'Lead Belly' Ledbetter. As he got into the life and times of this extraordinary character, he realised how much he owed his granddad. Not only had he encouraged his guitar playing, but he had also been the one who always told him as a youngster: 'Reading is the gateway to knowledge.' Granddad George had taught himself to read, as well as to play the banjo, while sailing all over the world, and said that his job had given him the best of everything—reading and travel. As usual, he had a punchline. 'It has,' he joked, 'made my mind broader than my arse.'

The Huddie Ledbetter story read like something out of the overactive imagination of a Hollywood scriptwriter. There was a story that he got his 'Lead Belly' nickname because he had gunshot in his stomach, but Eric had read that this was more than likely a myth and that it was just a simple play on his surname. Eric learned that Ledbetter had been born in Louisiana in 1889, the only child of poor share-croppers. It was after moving to Leigh in Texas, where an uncle taught him how to play an accordion, that he started to show musical talent. By the time he was in his teens he was able to play a range of instruments by ear, including the piano, harp, mandolin, harmonica and, notably, a twelve-string guitar.

Ledbetter—already known by his

nickname Lead Belly—had fathered two illegitimate children before he was eighteen, and had left home after bashing his drunken father over the head with a poker during an argument. He wandered the south-west States, with his twelve-string guitar as a constant companion, and picked up extra cash as a bar and street singer to go with wages earned as a cotton picker and labourer on the railroads.

In Dallas he became the 'seeing eyes' of renowned blues singer 'Blind' Lemon Jefferson, and under his influence developed a unique rhythmic guitar style.

Eric realised, while reading the Lead Belly life story, why his grandfather had been so drawn to him. As well as blues music, they shared a passion for drink—lakes of it.

Lead Belly was continually getting himself in trouble through his boozing, and was frequently thrown into jail. Following one sentence for allegedly assaulting a prostitute, he escaped from a chain gang and spent two years on the run under the alias 'Walter Boyd'.

While on the run, in 1918 he shot and killed a man in self-defence, and was sentenced to thirty years' hard labour in the Texas Shaw State Prison. The governor of the prison, Patrick Neff, was impressed by his guitar playing and singing, and got him to entertain the inmates. During one concert, he slipped in a song he had composed specially for the ears of the governor, cheekily asking him to 'be good 'n' kind and set me free'.

The governor was moved by this and granted a pardon, but within five years Lead Belly was back behind bars. This time he had been found guilty of knifing a white man after he had been pushed off the sidewalk and told: 'This ain't no place for niggers. You've gotta walk in the road.'

It was while an inmate at Louisiana State prison in 1934 that Lead Belly was introduced to John Lomax and his son, Alan. They were touring the south collecting work songs, ballads and spirituals for the Library of Congress.

They were recording songs on an Edison cylinder recording machine, and could not believe the amount of music that flowed from Lead Belly. He knew more than five hundred songs, many of them self-composed, and the rest he picked up by listening to singers in the cotton fields, in the prisons and on the railroads. He was a walking, singing, strumming library of African-American music.

Authorities at the Library of Congress were so impressed by the reports coming back to them from the Lomaxes that they loaned them a state-of-the-art acetate disc recorder, the forerunner of tape recorders. Lead Belly was encouraged to sit in front of the recorder and sing his heart out. Among the recordings that were later released on 78rpm records were his biggest hits 'Goodnight Irene' and 'Midnight Special', and, of course, 'Rock Island Line'.

The Lomaxes told the prison governor that Huddie Ledbetter should have been treated as a national treasure rather than as a murderer, and played him another song that Huddie had composed pleading for his freedom. Lead Belly succeeded again, and was granted a second pardon. The governor insisted it had less to do with the song than with the fact that the Lomaxes were ready to put their faith in Ledbetter's vow to be a 'good, peaceful and law-abidin' citizen'.

To show his thanks, Lead Belly volunteered to become chauffeur to John and Alan Lomax, and during their cross-country travels he became the singing star of their presentations on the history of American music.

John Lomax briefly took over as his manager, but Lead Belly objected to having to wear his prison clothes on stage and felt he was being used as a novelty act rather than an artist. Lomax later revealed that he decided he and Lead Belly should go their separate ways after the hot-tempered singer had pulled a knife on him during a quarrel when the singer was drunk. He liked to be a dandy dresser, and after switching management he became a hit on the New York folk singers' circuit. He also drew interest from the social set as a character, often performing at the swanky Café Society club.

Celebrating his freedom, Lead Belly took a bride twenty years his junior, and tried to make himself look younger by dyeing his white hair black. It was his second marriage, and it was not clear whether he had ever got round to divorcing his first wife, whom he had married in his teens.

Ledbetter earned little money from his records, which did not become massive sellers until after his death in 1949. He was found to have a rare neuromuscular disease in Paris while on a singing tour of Europe.

He composed his own obituary. 'If anyone asks you people, Who made up this song? Tell them it was Huddie Ledbetter. Done been here, and done gone.'

Eric was so engrossed in the Lead Belly life story that he spent almost an entire night reading, and was jolted out of his trip into the past by the sound of loud music. He looked out of his porthole at a band on the wharfside welcoming the *Britannic* to the United States for the last time.

They had arrived in New York.

CHAPTER FOUR

Carrying Bessie in one hand and a hold-all in the other, Eric caught the bus from Pier 90 at the Hudson Docks end of West 50th Street. He looked out in wonder at the passing panorama of New York City as he travelled to the Vanderbilt YMCA on East 47th Street, where he had a bed booked for three nights.

New York quickly cast its spell over Eric, as it had done to millions of visitors before him. He was awestruck as he looked up at the skyscrapers that seemed to disappear into the heavens. The New York skyline had first entranced him from his one-and-ninepenny seat at the Everton Picture Palace when he was a child and he had dreamed of being there ever since. He was a member of the movie-going generation, before television took over as the window on the world.

The plan Eric had worked out with his granddad was that he would spend a month searching for and riding the Rock Island Line. He would work his passage back to Liverpool from down in New Orleans aboard the cotton-carrying cargo ship, the *Quton*, which was owned by one of his grandfather's old seagoing pals.

His idea was to spend three days in New York before travelling from Central Station to Chicago, where he would switch to a Rock Island Line train. Eric had learned through many visits to his local library in Liverpool that the line had its roots in Chicago. The first iron rails, imported from England, were laid in the 1850s for an overland link between the Mississippi and Illinois rivers. The infant town of Rock Island was at the end of the line. The first Rock Island Line train took the same name as Robert Stephenson's pioneering steam-engine: *Rocket*.

Now, just over one hundred years later, the line had spread north, south, east and west like the tentacles of an octopus, and stretched from Illinois across Colorado, Iowa, Kansas, Missouri, Nebraska, New Mexico, Oklahoma and Texas. Southernmost reaches were to Galveston in Texas, and Eunice, Louisiana, while going north the Rock Island Line got as far as Minneapolis, Minnesota. They had all come across as magical names to Eric as he sat in the library reading room, feeling a tingle of excitement like a little boy the night before Christmas. He had read about it all. Now he was about to experience yet another of the great joys of reading—putting the words into action.

The Vanderbilt was hardly the most luxurious place in the world, but at just $3 a night it was good value, and the bunk-bed room he had to himself was a spacious paradise after the suffocating confinement of the ship's cabin. And a big bonus was that after breakfast in the cafeteria he did not have to wash up!

Making every minute count, he crammed in as much sightseeing as he could. He went to the top of the Empire State Building, took the ferry to Ellis Island, climbed up inside the Statue of Liberty, and lunched among the bohemians in Greenwich Village. He marvelled at the artistry of their street-painting exhibitions, and envied the talent of jazz and classical musicians on virtually every corner.

He also treated himself to a visit to Birdland. This was the home of 'cool' be-bop jazz, where he listened to the high-flying solos of the trumpeter Dizzy Gillespie and the deep-throated sounds of baritone sax-player Gerry Mulligan. But, much as he admired their dazzling musicianship, Eric felt they were often in danger of disappearing with a flash and a bang with their way-out improvisation.

On the evening of Eric's second day in New York, he learned a new word that his granddad had not taught him. *Mugging*. After aimlessly wandering round Times Square he headed down a side road, hoping to get some protection from a biting November wind that was cutting through his black woollen duffel coat. A stranger, wearing a trilby hat with the brim over his eyes and a muffler round his face, stepped in front of him and asked the time.

As Eric looked at his wristwatch, the man said, 'Now hand over the watch . . .'

In his hand the robber had a flick-knife.

Eric needed no more encouragement. He handed over the Newmark watch his mother had given to him eight months earlier for his twentieth birthday.

'Now all your cash,' the man said.

Eric reached into his pocket and emptied twelve dollars and seventeen cents into the man's hands.

'That all you've got?'

Eric nodded. 'Swear to God,' he lied.

With surprising politeness, the man said, 'Thank you, brother.' He seemed to want Eric to feel he had made a voluntary donation. Then, just as if to show the knife worked, he cut through the hood of Eric's duffel coat, and hurriedly walked off.

Eric resisted the temptation to chant in his direction: 'I fooled you ... I fooled you ... I've got all of two hundred and fifty more dollars ...'

Thanks to the advice of his travel-wise granddad, the cash—in fifty-dollar bills—was comfortably cushioning his feet inside his shoes.

As he walked back to Times Square, Eric came face to face with a

New York street cop, lounging on the corner of the side street having a crafty cigarette.

'I've just been robbed, officer,' he said. 'Thought I'd better report it.'

'Another mugging,' the cop said in a matter-of-fact way.

'Mugging?' said Eric, hearing the word for the first time.

'That's what we call it here,' the cop explained. 'Somebody picks you out as a mug and takes what he can. Was he a Caucasian?'

Another new word for Eric. 'A what?'

'Was he white, black, Hispanic?' the cop asked, struggling to show any real interest.

'Didn't get a proper look at him,' Eric said. 'Only telling you in case he picks on somebody else.' He held his hands wide apart, like an angler exaggerating his catch. 'He's got a knife this big—he could cut a rhino's throat with it.'

The cop was unimpressed. 'If you

want to make an official report,' he said, 'you'll have to go to the nearest police precinct, which is . . .'

As he started to point the way, Eric said: 'No, that's OK. He's welcome to my watch. Hope it gives him a good time. Thank you, officer.'

With that, Eric continued sightseeing. Many people would have been put off New York by the incident. But for him it was an experience that made his adventure all the richer. And he had the satisfaction of knowing he was still walking on money.

On his last day at the Vanderbilt YMCA, Eric got talking to a 22-year-old Californian student, who had dropped out of college to go on a motorcycle tour of the United States.

His name was Scott Wallace and he was the son of a Los Angeles lawyer who had threatened to disown him when he quit law school for the freedom of the road. With nostalgic memories of his 125cc Vespa, Eric understood exactly how he felt.

Once he clapped eyes on Scott's motorbike, he decided to embroider the facts about his Vespa a little, talking it up as a 250cc model. Even then, the magnificent bike that Scott was riding dwarfed it. He had a 750cc Harley Davidson XLCH Sportster that could purr to 100mph without clearing its throat.

Eric told him about his search for the Rock Island Line. 'You're searching for it?' Scott said, laughing. 'I didn't know it was lost.'

He and Eric got on really well, and within an hour of starting their conversation Scott had issued an invitation that Eric accepted without hesitation. 'It just so happens,' said Scott, 'that my next major stop is Chicago. Why not hitch a lift, and I'll take you right to where the Rock Island Line starts. It's only a spit past Chicago.'

They managed to fit Eric's holdall into a side compartment on the customised bike, but his guitar case had to be left behind. Bessie rode naked, strapped to his back, with just a cloth to protect her from the weather.

Eric felt as free as the wind as they left New York City behind them, bombing down the network of interstate highways and heading—in a roundabout way—for Chicago. What Scott had not told him was that he was taking the scenic route, dropping in on Philadelphia, Pittsburgh Pennsylvania, Cleveland in Ohio and then South Bend in Indiana, before making the final charge into Chicago, and then the little matter of another two hundred miles to Rock Island, Illinois. A 760-mile route had been stretched to much more than a thousand miles. Eric could hardly believe Scott's generosity in taking him along as a passenger on a guided tour of parts of America that he would have had no chance of seeing. It took them six days, mostly using YMCA hostels for their overnight stops.

It would have been five days, but they picked up—or, more accurately, were picked up by—a pair of sisters in a diner just outside Pittsburgh. They had an enjoyable, unscheduled stopover in a barn on a farm where the two girls worked. There were no complaints from Eric about the extra miles—and certainly no complaints about the night he spent in the barn! Between them, the sisters—both in their late teens—taught him things he had only read about in the adult books among his grandfather's collection.

The sisters were called Gertrude and Hilda, and were American-born daughters of a Norwegian farmer who had emigrated from Europe just before the Second World War. Eric was astonished at what they knew about sex, and how to get the most out of positions he hadn't even seen at Anfield! Hilda, the one he finished up with, mentioned a '69' and Eric thought it was some sort of ice cream. His sexual experiences had not gone much beyond a series of knee tremblers against the wall of the local pub.

When he mentioned to Hilda how surprised he was by her sexual knowledge, she told him it came from living on the farm. 'You'll be astonished what you can learn from the animals,' she explained. Eric smiled to himself, because 'Animals' to him meant a new rock group that he had heard was being formed in Newcastle. The Geordies were trying to catch up with the Mersey Beat.

Eric and Scott were finally exhausted by the sisters, who went off in search of new thrills.

As they neared the end of their journey, Eric made a vow to himself that one day he would buy a Harley Davidson. It had been like riding a magnificent wild beast, and he was not thinking about Hilda. As he and

Scott prepared to part company in Rock Island, he promised to give him the same VIP treatment if ever he visited Liverpool. He made a mental note not to offer him a ride on a Vespa.

Scott left him to 'get your ticket at the station for the Rock Island Line'. As Scott roared off on his Harley, Eric found himself regretting that he would no longer enjoy the freedom of the road with a great companion who was taking life by the horns and riding the hell out of it. But now he was going to have the freedom of the railroad to cheer him up. He was about to swap the two wheels of a Harley for the thundering wheels of a Rock Island Line Rocket.

CHAPTER FIVE

Abbey Station in the Illinois town of Rock Island looked from the outside more like a grand town hall than a railway station, with an eighty-foot clock tower rising from the centre of the red-tiled roof. Eric went through the elegant arched entrance and found himself in a ticket office area that had a chandelier and a polished floor so clean you could have eaten off it.

'And where are you off to today, young man?' asked a friendly, white-haired ticket clerk, who might have stepped out of a painting by Norman Rockwell, a famous painter of everyday American scenes.

Eric explained that he wanted to travel wherever he could on the Rock Island Line, and finally end up in New Orleans.

'Well, you're spoilt for choice, young man,' said the ticket clerk. 'There's the Rocky Mountain Rocket that takes you from Chicago through Omaha, Lincoln, Denver and on down to Colorado Springs. Lovely at this time of year.'

Eric found himself almost salivating, as if he were listening to a menu being read out at the Liverpool Adelphi, the poshest hotel in his home city.

'Then,' continued the clerk, 'we have the Corn Belt Rocket. That'll take you from Chicago through Des Moines and down into Kansas. Or you can take the Twin Star Rocket through Minneapolis, St Paul, Des Moines, Kansas City, Oklahoma City and on down into the Lone-star State of Texas and onto Fort Worth, Dallas and Houston.'

The clerk was talking with a rhythm that could almost have been set to Rock Island Line music.

'Of course, there's the Zephyr Rocket that heads through Burlington and down to St Louis,' he added, enjoying showing off his knowledge of the company trains. 'Or perhaps you prefer the Choctaw Rocket, which speeds you down through Memphis, Little Rock,

Oklahoma City and on into Amarillo in the heart of the Texas Panhandle. You'll have to make quite a few changes before you arrive at New Orleans, but I promise you'll get there in the end.'

Eric smiled to himself as he thought of asking for a ticket at Liverpool Lime Street, and getting the information: 'The train will be calling at Birmingham New Street, Coventry, Watford Junction and King's Cross.' Somehow that could not compete with the appetising ring of Memphis-Little Rock-Oklahoma City-Amarillo. He decided that it sure as hell was easier to write lyrics for an American railroad song than an English one—unless your name was John Betjeman, a wonderfully rhythmic poet whose writing about the English railways Eric had been introduced to by, naturally, his well-read granddad.

'I'll tell you what I can do for you,' the clerk said after thoughtfully studying a fistful of timetables. 'For fifty dollars, I can sell you a rover ticket, which will enable you to ride on any Rock Island Rocket train, anywhere, for the next month. Hundreds of miles and a choice of fourteen states for just fifty bucks. How does that suit you? And for you, young man, I'll make it first class all the way.' The ticket clerk coughed, almost in embarrassment. 'You might wonder why I'm so keen to help you,' he said. 'Y'see, I have a grandson travelling round Europe at this very moment, just like you are here seeing America. I only hope he's being looked after, like I'm trying to look after you.'

Eric excused himself, and went to the gentlemen's toilet. He took off his right shoe and peeled off a fifty-dollar bill. Five minutes later he had a travel-anywhere ticket in his hand, Bessie strapped to his back, his hold-all in his other hand and was off to Platform One to catch the Rocky

Mountain Rocket. First stop, Chicago.

He felt his eyes stinging with tears as he started off on his first journey, sitting comfortably in a first-class carriage—or car, as it was called in the States—pulled by one of the last steam-powered engines. It was painted Liverpool red and had a distinctive, streamlined yellow nose. In no time at all it had picked up speed and was rocketing along with true 'Rock Island Line' rhythm. Eric could almost have sung along to the beat of the wheels hurtling over the track, with a window on the American landscape to give him a stunning picture to go with the train's thrilling tempo.

Eric rode the trains for three weeks, criss-crossing states and time zones, and taking overnight breaks at Minneapolis, Omaha, Kansas City, Oklahoma City, Colorado Springs and Amarillo, where he bought himself jeans, shirts, cowboy boots and a stetson hat.

In Oklahoma City he turned on the television in his hotel room to find Olympic gold-medallist boxer Cassius Clay making his professional debut in his hometown of Louisville. He comfortably won on points and told the television audience in his after-fight interview: 'Keep watching my progress, folks, 'cos I am the greatest.'

Eric, who had been taught to box by former pro, Granddad George, felt that Clay was a bit young to make these claims, but could not think of a more talented heavyweight. That included the current world champion Floyd Patterson, who had made history six months earlier by becoming the first boxer to regain the world heavyweight title, after knocking out the Swedish Ingemar Johansson.

The one scar on Eric's adventure ride was that the farther south he went, the more he became aware of a colour bar: the separation of black people from white people. It made him feel sick to the stomach. Blacks were treated like third-class citizens, and he hated seeing 'whites only' restaurants, segregated toilets and buses, in which blacks had to sit at the back and give up their seat if a white passenger was standing. He knew that John Kennedy had a huge challenge facing him, but there was a mood of optimism among the fair-minded Americans Eric met on his travels. They thought that JFK was the man who could push through controversial Civil Rights laws.

Eric got extremely and loudly drunk on the train one day with a horde of Iowa Hawkeyes football fans, who were celebrating a victory over their deadly rivals from Notre Dame, Indiana. Every one of them had a whiskey flask, and they were very generous in passing the booze around. They had friendly arguments with Eric about the merits of soccer versus American football, and they fell about laughing when he passed on the famous quote of Liverpool manager Bill Shankly: 'Some people think football is a matter of life and death. I can assure them it's much more important than that.'

Another afternoon he got talking to a potato farmer from Iowa, who took a big interest in his guitar. Eric explained about his fascination with the 'Rock Island Line' lyrics, and the farmer asked him to sing the song as he knew it.

A little shy, but gaining in confidence as the farmer tapped his foot in rhythm with the song, he strummed Bessie as he sang the Lonnie Donegan version.

'You know those are not the only words to that song,' the farmer said. 'You'll find there are different lyrics to the spoken part according to which state you're in on the Rock Island Line.'

'Which version do you know?'

asked Eric, thinking he was going to get the Huddie Ledbetter one.

'The one we know here in Iowa,' said the farmer, 'revolves round the first ever train robbery by the Jesse James gang.'

Eric's mouth made goldfish movements, with no words coming out: he was that surprised. Yet another staggering fact about the Rock Island Line.

'When was that?' he managed to ask.

'It was back in the summer of 1873,' the farmer told him. 'It happened at Adair, just down the line from here. The gang used a rope to pull a rail loose as the Rock Island train came to the top of a steep climb. The engineer, a white man called John Rafferty, spotted the rope and the moving rail, and put the train into a sudden reverse. The engine shuddered and came off the track, rolled over and poor Rafferty was crushed to death.'

Eric could hardly believe what he was hearing. But nobody could have made this up.

The farmer continued: 'The James gang, who had been terrorising banks, escaped with hundreds of dollars from the train's safe, and cleaned out the most prosperous looking of the passengers. From then on they concentrated on train robberies rather than looting banks.'

'And you've heard this story as a song sung to the Rock Island Line tune?' Eric asked.

'Sure have,' said the farmer. 'The chorus is the same as you sing it, but the spoken verse is all about the James gang. It went something like . . .' He signalled for Eric to start strumming.

Now this here's the story about the
    Rock Island Line
And of the day in '73 the James
    gang robbed the train
As it slow-hauled its way up a

steep incline
With the mighty Rocket engine
    taking the full strain

As the gang lay in waiting and
    pulled away a rail
Brave engineer Rafferty tried to
    turn the train around
But his courageous effort was
    tragically to fail
As the engine rolled over crushing
    him to the ground

The James gang! The James gang!
They've hit the banks. Now they're
    hitting the trains
The James gang!

While the gallant engineer
    Rafferty lay a-dying
The cowardly James gang cleared
    out all the cash
And rode off, leaving our hero
    there a-lying
With blood on their hands and
    blood on their stash

To many Jesse James has become
a folk hero
But for those who prefer good
men like Rafferty on top
It's time to accept that he and his
gang are subzero
And the glorifying of the James
boys just has to stop
Yes siree, it just has to stop

Now the Rock Island Line is a
mighty good road
Oh the Rock Island Line is the
road to ride
The Rock Island Line is a mighty
good road
Well if you want to ride you gotta
ride it like you find it
Get your ticket at the station of
the Rock Island Line

Oh dear Lord hear our prayer
Let the good John Rafferty rest in
peace
Oh dear Lord hear our prayer

Let our memory of him never cease

The farmer told Eric how for a month after the death of Rafferty, the Rock Island engines were decorated with black ribbons in remembrance. Huge rewards were offered for the capture of Jesse James—dead or alive—but it was another eight years and several train robberies later before he was shot dead.

'James died a hero in many people's eyes,' said the farmer. 'Even President Theodore Roosevelt referred to him as America's Robin Hood. Here in Iowa we think of poor John Rafferty.'

Eric asked the farmer what he knew about Huddie Ledbetter's version of 'Rock Island Line'.

'We've got a young country singer over here called Johnny Cash,' he said, 'and he sings a similar version, which refers to the same accident that happened on the line. Rock Island Line has one of the best safety records in the world. The only major accident that I know of was when a bridge was washed away in the Colorado floods of 1929. Ten people were killed that day when the Stratton railway bridge crashed into the river, taking several carriages of the Rock Island Rocket with it.'

The farmer seemed a warm, likeable man, but as he was leaving he said something that worried Eric. It made him wonder again about the racial tensions building across the United States. 'When you get down south,' the farmer said before leaving the carriage at Des Moines, 'don't let them tell you that's a nigger song. White country singers like Johnny Cash and Pete Seeger have all got claims on it. It ain't jazz. It's white folk music. Black guys like Ledbetter and that Lonnie Donegan stole it from white singers.'

Eric wanted to tell him that

Lonnie Donegan was white and Scottish, but he realised there was no point. He now knew the true meaning of another word he had learned—*bigot*.

You wouldn't get racism like that in Britain, Eric thought, a little smugly, as the train continued on its clickety-clack way into the Deep South. Then he recalled that not that long ago—in the summer of 1958—the streets of London had run red with blood during the Notting Hill race riots. White fascist thugs, chanting racist slogans, had attacked West Indian immigrants. The riots had raged for five days and nights, and it was because of this that the Notting Hill Carnival was launched the following year to help ease the tension.

Racism, Eric realised, was a worldwide disease.

On the last lap of his tour, as he got close to New Orleans, Eric heard yet another twist in the story of the

Rock Island Line.

A veteran black conductor checked his ticket, and asked in a friendly way his reason for visiting the home of jazz. When Eric told him he was seeking facts about the lyrics of Huddie Ledbetter's song 'Rock Island Line', he asked: 'Who told you that was Lead Belly's song?'

'My granddad,' said Eric. 'He's got Lead Belly's original recording, made back in 1934.'

'Well, with greatest respect to your gran' pappy,' the conductor said, 'he doesn't know what he's talking about. Sure, Lead Belly recorded "Rock Island Line", but—take it from me—he did not compose it. He first heard it when he was in prison, and the man he heard singing it was Kelly Pace, who was serving five years for burglary. This was in the early thirties.'

Eric had never heard of Kelly Pace. 'You seem pretty certain about it,' he told the conductor.

'I sure am,' he said. 'You see, I was in that same prison in Arkansas with Kelly Pace. It was known as Cummins Farm Prison. I was young and headstrong, and got a stretch in prison for shooting a guy who had made a play for my gal. Anyway, Kelly used to sing unaccompanied—a cappella, it's called—and would get us other prisoners joining in. They were what were known as "negro call songs". Pace would sing the first melody line and the rest of us would repeat it with harmonies, or respond with a second line. For instance, if he sang "The Rock Island Line is a mighty fine road", we would answer with, "Yes, the Rock Island Line *is* a mighty fine road". We would get a rhythm going and chop wood or break up rocks in unison as we sang. You'd be surprised how much easier it made the work. If you ever see a film of US Marines drilling, you will hear them using the same rhythm-calling method. And it's Kelly Pace who deserves all the credit.'

Eric was fascinated. 'So how come Huddie Ledbetter recorded it as if it was *his* song?' he asked.

'He came back to the prison farm with those song collectors John and Alan Lomax, who were tracing the roots of American music,' the conductor explained. 'He heard us harmonising on the "Rock Island Line", with Kelly Pace doing the lead singing. Lead Belly, who was one helluva guitarist by the way, later recorded the song for the Lomaxes, singing it solo and putting his own stamp on it. He sang it like it had never been sung before, but don't go giving him the credit for composing it. That song grew out of the prisons.'

The conductor suddenly looked out of the window. 'Wow, I'd best be going,' he said. 'We're just twenty minutes or so from New Orleans. You're going to love it. I know it. Have a great Christmas. Bye.'

Christmas! Eric had been so

wrapped up in his train trip that he had completely forgotten the time of year. The Rock Island Rocket was pulling into Union Station, New Orleans. It was the day before Christmas Eve, 1960, and he was at the end of the Rock Island Line.

CHAPTER SIX

Christmas in New Orleans was one long party. Eric knew it was going to be fun the moment he checked into the YMCA hostel on historic Canal Street, where he was greeted by a desk clerk dressed as Santa Claus. 'Welcome to New Aulins,' he said, using one of the many ways people had of pronouncing the city's name. 'We want to bring the spirit of Christmas that you know at home here to our hostel. It's our aim to make all our guests feel part of our large Christian family. Please have a

71

very, very Merry Christmas with us.'

The hostel was festooned with Christmas decorations that almost hid the fact that it was a tired, 1890s building in need of several licks of paint. The interior was spotlessly clean, and Eric had a small but cosy room that overlooked the rear of a honky-tonk bar from where a boogie-woogie piano could be heard non-stop.

It would usually have been considered a nuisance to have continual noise in the background, but this was New Orleans, where the sounds of jazz came with the air everyone breathed.

Eric could not believe his ears when he walked from the hostel through the heart of the French Quarter. In every bar and restaurant and on every street corner there were people making music. It was mostly traditional New Orleans jazz, but there were lots of rhythm 'n' blues, Latin combos, harmonica-playing sidewalk dancers, swinging sextets, quiet quartets, singing duos, gospel choirs and just about every combination you could think of.

Even in the road there was music as a traditional New Orleans funeral procession passed by. It was led by an undertaker wearing a top hat, twirling a yellow umbrella and dancing with enormous energy to the sound of a brass band marching ahead of the cortège. Two black horses draped in black velvet ribbons were pulling the hearse, which was a flower-decked, glass-sided, rubber-wheeled coach. Eric thought that it was almost worth dying here in New Orleans just to get that sort of send-off.

He walked the length of Bourbon Street, stopping to watch a parade of street performers—dancers, singers, acrobats, magicians and contortionists—and then moved on down to the quayside to look at the paddle steamers heading to and fro across the Mississippi.

It was from Julia Street docks, just a mile away from here, that he would be heading for home two days before New Year's Eve. He had scheduled to meet his granddad's old friend Tom Riley, the captain of the *Quton* cargo ship, on 29 December to discuss his duties on the voyage back to Liverpool. As he looked out across the Mississippi he found himself thinking of the Mersey, which was little more than a puddle compared with this mighty river. He suddenly felt his first pang of homesickness, wondering what his mum, dad and granddad were doing for Christmas. He had sent them postcards and letters from almost every stop he had made, so that when he got home he would have a sort of diary of his trip.

Liverpool seemed a million miles away. He would miss the traditional Boxing Day football match, the singing of carols by the Kop choir at

Anfield, drinking with his mates at the Halfway House in Scotland Road—American beer was piss compared with the mild-and-bitter at home—and, most of all, he would miss that warm, hugging atmosphere of Christmas Day when pressies were opened and the house filled with the aroma of his mum's once-a-year turkey dinner cooking.

As he stood looking down into the waters of the Mississippi, Eric quietly laughed to himself at the memory of the Christmas dinner two years ago when Granddad George had come home, boozed from the Halfway House, and fallen asleep at the dinner table. His face dropped into a dish of gravy, and as he jolted upright again he thought he'd just had his meal and said to Eric's mum, 'That was very nice, thank you, love. A little less gravy next time.'

Just as Eric was slipping into a rare depression, his homesickness was overtaken by a different sort of pang—hunger. It was time to get back to the hostel for his dinner.

By the time he returned to the YMCA his ears were ringing from all the different sounds he had been listening to. He thought Liverpool was a musical city, but compared with New Orleans it was as quiet as an empty church.

There was a bonus waiting for him. Girls from the YWCA had been invited to join the boys for dinner, and he found himself seated opposite a couple from Vancouver. The girl was stunningly beautiful and Eric found himself feeling jealous of her partner, who introduced himself as Max.

'And this is Grace,' he added.

'Amazing, Grace,' Eric said lamely.

'Very original,' Grace said.

Eric was embarrassed about his clumsy attempt at humour, and tried to concentrate on a 'shrimp Creole' that seemed to have the limbs of lobsters in it. If this was their shrimp, what were their prawns like?

Grace refused to let him sink into silence, and kept hitting him with questions.

'What d'you do for a living?'

'I'm, uh, in between jobs. I was in sales but now I'm travelling the world looking for new opportunities.'

'What did you used to sell?'

'Uh, Vespa scooters . . . you know, those little Italian jobs that are all the craze with students in Europe.'

'What are your hobbies?'

'Football and, uh, the guitar.'

'You play?'

'No, I watch. Liverpool, the best team in the world.'

'No, I meant the guitar. Do you play?'

'Well, I thought I did until I came here to New Orleans. Now I know that I'm strictly an amateur.'

'I think you're being modest.'

Eric was getting uncomfortable. She was totally ignoring Max and focusing all her attention on him.

But they seemed a well-suited couple. He studied them between chewing shrimp and sipping Californian wine. Max was as handsome as hell, all smoothness and style in immaculate blue jeans and matching shirt. He had blond hair that was down almost to his shoulders, and he wore a row of beads tight round his neck. Eric reckoned he was a couple of years older than the smashing girl at his side, who seemed to be about his own age.

Eric could see why Max was happy to be with Grace. She wore a flowing, floral dress, little make-up, had two long strings of beads dangling over small yet enticing breasts, and her long brown hair matched the colour of her eyes, which sparkled as she laughed her way through the meal. She would be perfectly at home with the soon-to-be-fashionable hippies. Eric thought she was the most beautiful girl he had ever seen.

She kept pumping him for information. 'Why d'you dress like a cowboy?'

'Uh, I bought this gear in Amarillo a few days ago. Thought it looked the business.' Eric sensed himself blush under her gaze.

'Have you a girlfriend pining at home in Liverpool?'

Eric laughed to himself.

'Not exactly pining,' he said. 'I've told her to get on her bike.'

Grace's pretty forehead knotted. 'What does that mean, "on her bike"?'

'It's just an expression we use when you want somebody to sort of move on. I've given her what the Spanish call the old El Bow.'

Grace laughed. 'You talk in a peculiar way,' she said. 'But I find it kind of cute.'

'It's pure Scouse,' explained Eric. 'We Scousers, people from Liverpool, talk with a nasal twang that was handed down to us from the

Gods of Mount Sinus.'

'I don't know what you're talking about,' Grace said, her brown eyes suddenly wide. 'But I love listening to you!'

After the huge main course of Cajun jambalaya had been tackled and tamed, Max leaned over and pecked Grace on the cheek.

'See you later, Sis,' he said. 'I'm off to chase that girl I met on the paddle steamer yesterday.'

Eric was startled, flustered and delighted all at once. Sis! So all this time she had been chatting him up, and he had had no idea. What a turnip, he thought.

Grace laughed like crazy when Eric confessed he thought Max was her boyfriend. 'I thought you were being a bit cold and abrupt with your answers,' she said. 'I know Englishmen are supposed to lack passion, and so I just took it that you were typical of your breed.'

Eric spent the next three days (and

nights) proving to Grace that Englishmen—well, Scousers at least—were anything but lacking in passion. It was under one of the mature oak trees in City Park that they shared their first kiss. It was long and clinging, and Eric experienced for the first time in his life the quickening of the pulse that accompanies that little thing called love.

This was not wham-bang lust like he had experienced with Hilda. This was all tenderness, affection, soft cuddles and gentle caressing. They walked hand in hand through the streets of New Orleans, soaking up the Christmas carnival atmosphere and enjoying every second of being in each other's company.

The combination of the magical mood of the jazz capital of the world and being with the sort of girl he would normally have only dreamed about gave Eric a feeling almost of light-headedness. He felt as if he were floating along the boulevards of New Orleans. And he sensed that Grace felt the same.

At twenty-one, she was a couple of months older than him. She and Max were both on a Christmas break from university, where she was studying modern history. They had come to New Orleans on a jazz pilgrimage. Max played the clarinet and admired the style of the old masters Johnny Dodds and George Lewis. Eric was more interested in the style of his sister.

Not only was Grace intelligent, but she had the sort of bubbly personality that radiated happiness and confidence, which instantly spread to Eric. He had never felt so comfortable in a girl's company. Grace was of a type that Eric would have expected to be out of his league, but he impressed her with his wide-ranging knowledge. It was all just bits and pieces he had picked up reading his granddad's books. Good old Granddad! Good old books!

Eric was surprised and quietly proud to find that university-educated Grace was in some way in awe of *him*. 'I really admire your courage and independence,' she told him. 'Not many people your age would have the strength of character to take on the challenge of a solo trip across the world. It's the sort of thing I would love to do when I leave university.'

It made Eric realise that he had matured in the few short weeks since he had set sail from Liverpool. He had gone off in search of the Rock Island Line, and had discovered himself. And he had found Grace.

They gave each other little presents on Christmas Day as if they had known each other for months rather than just hours. He bought her an amethyst bracelet from a street seller, who swore it would bring lasting love and luck both to the one who bought it and the one who wore it. She gave him a key ring that had a miniature guitar hanging from it.

Eric and Grace cuddled each other and cried on Boxing Day evening when it was time for her to leave. She and Max had arranged to be back in Vancouver to see the New Year in. They exchanged addresses, telephone numbers and words of undying love. Eric could not believe he had used the 'love' word. He put it down to the romantic atmosphere of New Orleans, but after he had waved Grace and Max away on the Greyhound bus he knew that he really was in love. Now he was homesick *and* love-sick.

Feeling low the next day, Eric went into a Bourbon Street bar and drank so many red rum Hurricanes that his legs suddenly felt as if they were on springs. As he left the bar he impulsively called into the tattooist's parlour next door and asked if he knew what a Liverbird looked like.

A drunk Scouser trying to describe a Liverbird to a French-speaking Creole was like something out of a Jacques Tati comedy film. Eric slurring in heavy Scouse 'like they have on the Liverpool shirts' did little to end the confusion.

'What is a "shairt"?' the tattooist asked carefully.

He finally produced a book of birds and animals, and Eric selected what he thought was a dragon as being the closest to a Liverbird. It was tattooed in red on his inside left arm, alongside the one word 'Liverpool'.

So it was that a heavily hungover Eric woke up the next morning to find he had 'Liverpool' tattooed on his arm alongside a stork. But he was happy enough with it, and went back to the parlour to have the words 'Rock Island Line' tattooed on the inside of his right arm. As a bonus, the tattooist added a good likeness of a Rock Island Rocket engine.

Granddad 'Signpost' George would have been proud of him.

Eric kept his date with *Quton* captain Tom Riley, who turned out to be a fellow Scouser. Now in his fifties, Tom had worked with Eric's granddad when he first went to sea as a fifteen-year-old, and talked warmly about 'Signpost' as if he had been a father figure.

'It's up to you what you do on the trip home, young Eric,' he said. 'You can have a nice easy ride if you wish. But if you've got any of your granddad in you, I know you'll want to pull your weight.'

'I wouldn't dream of bumming a trip home,' Eric said. 'I'm ready to work my Niagara Falls off.'

Riley laughed at the rhyming slang. 'You've borrowed that from a Cockney,' he said, fingering a huge, lumpy scar down the right side of his face that Eric had been trying to ignore. 'Don't worry, pal, I don't like to look at it either. I got it in a ship's fire a few years back. The doctors keep trying to persuade me to have plastic surgery, but I like—to use Cockney rhyming slang again—my old boat race.' He laughed as he added: 'And I'll tell you what, young Eric, it's a turn-on for the ladies.'

They shook hands like old friends, and Eric felt excited at the thought of returning to the sea as he walked back to the Canal Street YMCA for what was to be his last night in New Orleans.

It was during this walk that Eric found out—by pure coincidence— the real source of the Rock Island Line song.

He was passing a bar in South Rampart Street when he spotted a hand-painted notice that nearly took his breath away. It read: 'The home of skiffle . . . where it all started.'

This was the first time he had seen or heard any reference to skiffle since his arrival in the States. Eric wandered into the dingy, dimly lit bar to find a four-piece group ripping through an upbeat version of one of Lonnie Donegan's hit songs, 'Cumberland Gap'. There were fewer than a dozen customers, and most of them were more interested in their drinks than the music.

When the group took a break, Eric bought a drink for the lead singer, an elderly black man from New Orleans. He asked him about the birth of skiffle.

'It was right here in New Orleans,' he said. 'Right here in South Rampart Street more than seventy years ago. It became known as skiffle, but it's a mispronunciation of the original word "scuffle". Self-taught musicians used to scuffle for cents in the street, improvising with all sorts of instruments, such as combs, bottles, tea-chests and washboards. It became known as jugband music, and they used to play at rent-raising parties where everyone except the musicians has to pay money to help with the rent.'

Eric bought him a second drink. 'So why have I not heard the word skiffle since I came here?' he asked.

'Because it just went out of use,' the old jazzman said with a shrug. 'Crazily, it's just becoming popular again because some Brit called Donny Lonegan or something has had a hit over here with "Rock Island Line".'

'Lonnie Donegan,' said Eric.

'That's the guy,' the veteran said. 'What the hell would a Brit know about the "Rock Island Line"?'

'He borrowed the song from Huddie Ledbetter,' Eric said, showing off his new knowledge.

'That wasn't Lead Belly's song,' the old man said firmly.

'He heard Kelly Pace singing it as a call-and-response song in prison,' Eric added.

'Wasn't a prison song either,' the old man said. 'Pace would have heard railroaders singing it. They were known as Gandy dancers—they worked for the Gandy rail company and were railroad layers. It was while laying the Rock Island Line that they first started singing the song, way back in the last century. The workers used to dance African-style and sing in rhythm as they laid the lines.'

Eric saw in his mind's eye the railway workers laying the lines to the rhythmic beat of 'Rock Island Line', and realised the story made sense.

'Don't pay no heed to people saying Lead Belly composed "Rock Island Line",' the veteran singer continued. 'He *adapted*, that's what he did. Just as he *adapted* his biggest hit song, "Goodnight Irene". That was based on a true story told way back in the last century about a man breaking up with his young wife, and getting suicidal about it. Black slaves in the cottonfields were the first to sing that one, not Huddie Ledbetter. Not Kelly Pace.'

The old musician tilted his head and finished his drink. 'And I'll tell you one more thing,' he said, preparing to rejoin the band back on their small stage. 'Nobody owns that Rock Island song, not Kelly Pace, not Lead Belly, and certainly not that Donnie whatshisname. "Rock Island Line" is a song that belongs to the people. It's a people's song.'

For the price of a third drink, Eric got the band to play their version of 'Rock Island Line'. He listened respectfully, and kept to himself that he preferred Lonnie Donegan's version.

The search for the story behind the 'Rock Island Line' was over. Now the sea—and home—were calling.

CHAPTER SEVEN

Eric saw in the New Year with Tom Riley and his crew, celebrating it by joining in the colourful carnival dance through the French Quarter. They should by now have been at sea, but thunder storms, engine problems and then a strike at the docks delayed their departure.

The strike was caused by another new word for Eric's growing vocabulary: *containerisation*.

Riley pointed to a huge ship that was filled with just one large container. 'That,' he said, 'is going to revolutionise cargo shipping, and will eventually put the docks out of business.'

'How come?' asked Eric, who had many friends and family working in the docks at Liverpool.

'It takes a tenth of the number of dockers to load and unload that container ship,' Riley explained. 'The guys on strike are in fear for their futures. If, as is sure to happen, containerisation catches on, docks all over the world will be hit, and many of them closed.'

Eric tried hard not to scoff at the suggestion. Liverpool without the docks, he thought. Why, that would be like Wembley Stadium without the Twin Towers.

It was 20 January 1961 when the *Quton* finally set sail, the very day that John F. Kennedy was sworn in as president and made his memorable 'ask not what your country can do for you, but what you can do for your country' speech.

Eric looked back from the deck of the *Quton* at the port of New Orleans with genuine sadness, and he knew that one day he would return to the city known as the Big Easy. It had won his heart in the same way as Grace had. With both of them, it had been love at first sight.

The *Quton* took a little longer to love. In fact, at first sight it was something closer to hate. Tom Riley explained that she had been built in the United States as a Liberty ship in the early years of the Second World

War, and originally had five holds that could carry 9,000 tons of cargo, with aeroplanes and tanks lashed to her deck. Nearly three thousand Liberty ships were built quickly for war service, and were sold off cheaply for cargo duties when peace was declared in 1945.

Riley gave Tom a tour of the ship, showing it off as proudly as a father with a new baby. But Eric got the impression it was more of a slumbering old man than a lively baby. The ship was 441 feet long and 56 feet wide, and had a three-cylinder steam engine and a speed of eleven knots. After the luxury of the *Britannic*, it was a rust bucket.

When Riley and his partners bought it in 1946, it had been restructured to four holds, which were now stacked with huge, plastic-protected bales of cotton. They had renamed the ship *Quton* from the Arabic for cotton. 'Bringing cotton from New Orleans to Britain made economic sense at the time,' Riley explained. 'Your granddad was the original first mate and served on board until his retirement. But we're now struggling to make profits because of the much cheaper cotton imports from India.'

In her golden days, the *Quton* had a crew of forty but this was now down to fourteen, plus—for this trip—Eric. He was determined not to be a dead weight and insisted he was happy to do the dirtiest job they could find him.

He accepted boiler-room duty, a job so hot and demanding that it was done in four-hour shifts shared with three other crew members. He became particularly friendly with Todd, an Australian who was working his way around the world by sea.

'Around the world in eighty days?' Eric had asked.

'No,' replied Todd. 'More like eight hundred days. I expect to be away from Oz for something like two years.'

Now that, thought Eric, was *real* adventuring.

The crew also took shifts in the crowded sleeping quarters, which had six bunk beds, two toilets and two shower cubicles. Eric soon learned how to use the noise and vibration of the engine as a rhythm to help him sleep. As he drifted off he reckoned it was almost like a skiffle beat.

Life on board was basic and primitive, yet Eric found that the camaraderie on the ship made up for the lack of amenities. He now fully understood the saying, 'Everybody's in the same boat'.

Once they got away from the Gulf of Mexico and into the Atlantic the temperature dropped, and Eric was pleased to have the heat of the boiler room to protect him from the dip to near-zero winter temperatures.

Tom Riley and his first mate, a

Swede called Olof, had their own private quarters close to the control room, and they shared four-hour-on four-hour-off watches. Strangely, the captain never slept in his cabin but always on the deck, where he had made a bed for himself from an old bedstead, which folded against the side of the ship. On top of the mattress he had fastened a sleeping bag.

When Eric asked why he didn't sleep in his comfortable cabin, he just shrugged and said, 'Claustrophobia, I guess.'

Riley was popular with his crew, which was like the United Nations. He and Eric were the only Brits, along with three Americans, three Cubans, two West Indians, two Mexicans, a French-Canadian, plus Sweden's Olof and Aussie Todd. They were all bound together by a love of the sea and travel.

The Atlantic was reasonably kind to them, apart from one bad, storm-tossed night when Eric wondered if they were going to lose their cargo of cotton or their lives. As the *Quton* pitched and rolled on the angry waves, nearly the entire crew suffered seasickness, with the exception, amazingly, of Eric.

'I see you've inherited your granddad's sea legs and stomach,' a green-faced Tom Riley told him. 'Never once did I see him giving in to seasickness. You're very lucky.'

Eric decided that Riley was truly mad. Throughout the storm he had remained in his makeshift bed out on the deck. It was amazing that he had not drowned.

He realised why Tom and his grandfather were so close. Not only were they both extremely eccentric, but they shared a huge appetite for reading. The captain's cabin was lined with books, including novels, war memoirs, celebrity biographies and many books of poetry. Riley loved quoting his favourites:

Rudyard Kipling's 'If', John Masefield's 'Cargoes', Edward Lear's 'The Owl and the Pussycat', Longfellow's *Hiawatha*, and Samuel Taylor Coleridge's *The Rime of the Ancient Mariner*.

'I hope you take after your granddad with your reading as well as your strong sea legs,' Riley said. 'He was the man who first encouraged me to read something more than just the back pages of newspapers. The greatest joy I know is to sit with my feet up on deck on a calm sea reading a good book. There's nothing to touch it.'

Riley told Eric that the first books that got him interested in reading were the Captain Hornblower adventures by C.S. Forester. 'You can almost taste the salt of the seawater when you're reading those books,' he said, relating stories of eighteenth-century sea battles as if he'd taken part in them.

'It was like opening the floodgates

for me. With your granddad pointing the way, I started to read a new book every week. First of all I read fiction and discovered the joy of reading great English authors like Dickens, Galsworthy and Hardy. Then I moved on to wonderful stories from American writers such as Hemingway, Steinbeck, Fitzgerald and Mark Twain.'

Riley was speaking as passionately as an evangelist seeking a new flock, but in Eric he was preaching to the converted. His grandfather had convinced him long ago that a kind of peaceful paradise could be found between the covers of books.

Riley did inspire Eric to take a deeper interest in poetry, and he spent much of his spare time on board the *Quton* reading Riley's vast collection of poems. He loved the rhythm of the writing, and sensed he could almost set the likes of Masefield and Milton to music. Eric quietly decided that once he was back on dry land he would start a poetry collection of his own.

On the night before docking at Liverpool at the end of the fourteen-day voyage, they had a rum-fuelled party at which Captain Riley narrated Kipling's 'Gunga Din', and Aussie Todd gave a rendering of Banjo Paterson's 'Boots', followed, naturally, by 'Waltzing Matilda'.

Eric brought Bessie up from his bunk bed and, of course, sang 'Rock Island Line'—the Lead Belly version.

The next morning they dropped anchor at Albert Dock, Liverpool. The adventure was over. Or was it just starting?

CHAPTER EIGHT

Eric had been away three months, but it seemed more like three years. His granddad had told him that travel would make him a different man, and he certainly felt that he had done some necessary growing up during his search for the Rock Island Line.

Granddad George gave him a hero's welcome home, and squeezed every memory of his trip from him as if, through Eric, he was trying to live the journey of discovery for himself. He was particularly keen to hear about his experiences aboard the *Quton*. 'I must have done that New Orleans–Liverpool run on her a hundred times,' he said, 'and I miss her like an old girlfriend who was bloody good in bed. She wasn't the most luxurious ship, but she had real character and it was a joy to work on her.'

He poured scorn on Eric's gloomy forecast that containers could put most of the Liverpool dockers out of work. 'You've got to be joking,' he said. 'Liverpool docks is the heartbeat of our great city. They will be thriving long after you and I have curled up our toes and fallen off the perch.'

Tom Riley reached a new peak in Eric's estimation when Granddad George revealed a little more of his history.

'I bet,' he said, 'that Tom didn't tell you why he sleeps on deck?'

'He told me it had to do with claustrophobia,' Eric said.

'Gollocks,' Granddad said. 'During the war the ship he was serving on was torpedoed. He was asleep in his cabin at the time. Shocked awake, he stumbled out on deck and then realised his best pal was still in the cabin. He battled back through the flames to rescue him, but after he had carried him out on his shoulder he was found to be dead.'

Eric shuddered at the horrible picture that came into his mind.

Granddad continued: 'Tom suffered severe burns, and has never been able to sleep in a cabin since. It was a nightmare that haunted him for years. The captain of his ship put his name forward for a medal, but he refused to accept it because he said he had let his pal down. That's the sort of guy Tom is. The most loyal man walking this earth . . . or sailing our seas.'

'A true hero,' said Eric. 'And he never once mentioned it. He was just happy to let us think he was mad for sleeping out on deck. What a man!'

Eric told his grandfather how Riley was still a keen reader, and that he was full of praise for Signpost, who had opened his eyes to how richly rewarding it could be.

'Tom deserves all the praise,' Granddad said. 'He was the one who had the sense to listen to me. I am always telling people they should read more, but I usually find deaf ears. Tom listened, took notice and was wise enough to start on the reading adventure that will last him a lifetime.'

The mood lightened when Eric

showed Granddad George his tattoos. He laughed like a drain. 'That Liverbird,' he said, 'looks like a bloody parrot.'

Eric left his granddad laughing and—with Bessie strapped to his back—went off to meet Terry Thompson and Alan Holmes at the Halfway House pub in Scotland Road. They listened with a mixture of envy and wonder to the stories of his trip, making him give graphic details of his stop-over with the sisters in the barn just outside Pittsburgh.

He kept to himself his meeting with Grace. She did not deserve their dirty, one-track minds going to work on her.

They were impressed by the detective work he had done on the birth of the 'Rock Island Line' song, and celebrated their reunion by playing the Lonnie Donegan version.

Inspired by his visit to New Orleans, Eric tried to encourage

Terry and Alan to give up their jobs and go full-time as skiffle group musicians. But they preferred to continue as semi-professionals, despite the fact that the Rock Island Skifflers were gradually building up a strong following in Liverpool.

Terry was a clerk in the docks, and Eric decided not to mention the container revolution heading his way—like a hurricane that would change thousands of lives. Alan was close to finishing his apprenticeship as a type compositor. Eric did not want to depress him by telling him about an article he had read in America. It stated that there were now 6,000 computers in use in the USA, and forecast that one of the things they would soon be able to do was set type for newspapers and magazines.

There was now an explosion of what had become known as the Mersey Beat, and there were dozens of groups battling to get recognition.

They included Hobo Rick and the City Slickers, who featured a know-all called Ricky Tomlinson on banjo. They were rivals to another skiffle group called the Mars Bars, which later developed into Gerry and the Pacemakers and moved away from skiffle to go down the rock road. They never walked alone from that moment on.

The Pacemakers, fronted by the bubbling Gerry Marsden, toured and explored the same Liverpool/ Hamburg circuit as another group that was causing ripples of excitement. They were called the Beatles, and Eric noted that two of them—John Lennon and Paul McCartney—had come from the skiffle school, where they had been known as The Quarrymen and then Johnny and the Moondogs. And he recalled that George Harrison had joined them just before they became the Beatles, but had been deported from Hamburg because he was too young for a work permit.

The thought of travelling to Hamburg and performing in the clubs out there appealed to Eric, but he knew there was no chance because Terry and Alan wanted steady income from their jobs.

The only breakthrough that would entice Terry and Alan to become full-time professionals was a recording contract, and as the Beatles had recently been turned down by Decca, what chance did the Rock Island Skifflers have?

As they came offstage after a gig at the Cavern, one of their fans pushed a *Liverpool Echo* into Eric's hands. 'You'll be interested in the story on page seven,' she said.

Eric turned to the article that was headlined, 'Liverpool bands wanted for recording dates.'

The story featured an interview with a Liverpool record-shop owner called Brian Epstein, who was looking for more local bands to join a stable he had just started by signing the Beatles.

He was holding auditions at the Adelphi Hotel, and Eric made a booking for him to hear the Rock Island group.

There were a dozen bands queuing to be heard, and it was seven hours before Eric and his pals were ushered into the suite where Epstein and two record producers were sitting behind a table at the back of the room.

'Just one song, please, chaps,' one of Epstein's companions said. 'We're all listened out.'

'That's encouraging,' Eric mumbled. 'Nothing like feeling welcome.'

They hammered out the Lead Belly version of 'Rock Island Line' in a room that had appalling acoustics and about as much atmosphere as a funeral parlour.

The silence at the end of it could have been measured in fathoms.

Finally, Brian Epstein cleared his throat and gave his judgement. 'I'm sorry to have to tell you, boys,' he said, 'that as well as you performed the song, skiffle is as dead as a dodo. Rock 'n' roll is where it's at.'

'Told you,' said Terry. 'A five-minute craze.'

As Eric walked towards the door, Epstein added: 'Excuse me, lead singer, I have to tell you I was very impressed by your narration delivery on that song. Have you thought of trying acting?'

Rock 'n' roll had won. Eric realised that Epstein was right. The skiffle revival had been and gone.

Yet he found that as he left the Adelphi he felt elated rather than disappointed. He knew now where his future lay.

That night he made a telephone call. 'Captain Riley,' he said, 'when does the *Quton* make its next run to New Orleans?'

Then he got out one of his

granddad's atlases, and worked out the route from New Orleans to Grace's home town of Vancouver.

POSTSCRIPT

In 1980 the Rock Island Line, knocked off the rails by cheap air flights, went into liquidation. It was the largest such bankruptcy in United States history.

AUTHOR'S NOTE

Thanks to my scriptwriter pal Norman Giller for helping me to get this adventure story from my head down on to paper.